The Little Book of Workplace Happiness

A little book solving the big problems of workplace culture

Anthony Poponi

Published by Caliente Press

1775 E. Palm Canyon Drive, Suite 110-198

Palm Springs, CA 92264

www.anthonypoponi.com

Book Layout ©2017 BookDesignTemplates.com

Ordering Information:

Quantity sales. Special discounts are available on quantity purchases by corporations, associations, and others. For details, contact the "Special Sales Department" at the address above.

The Little Book of Workplace Happiness/ Anthony Poponi. —1st ed.

ISBN 978-1-943702-27-5

"The most insightful resource on workplace happiness since the release of the documentary *Office Space*."

—ANN NONYMOUS

Author's Note: A#, as in I'm a sharp author—note received? #dadjokes

Author's Second Note: *The Little Book of Workplace Happiness* was originally going to be called *The Skinny Book of Workplace Happiness*, but the publisher thought it would confuse people, who might think it was a book on dieting at work. The publisher, who shall go unnamed, was eventually fired, but we incorporated their suggested change anyway.

Anthony Poponi is a happiness expert, energetic professional speaker, workplace consultant, and founder of Focus on the 40© programs and resources. He specializes in putting joy in our workplaces and in our communities through workshops and keynotes that leave his audiences buzzing and inspired to enact change. He's been called a father figure (dad bod) and is armed with a wide arsenal of dad jokes and world-class puns, even though he doesn't have any children. His blend of comedic wit and happiness expertise makes him a hard act to follow onstage.

Read more about Anthony at: www.anthonypoponi.com/about

For Canadian Users: www.anthonypoponi.com/aboot

THIS BOOK IS BEING TRANSLATED INTO 1,436 LANGUAGES, INCLUDING:

Pig Latin – Available-ay in-ay int-pray ater-lay is-thay ear-yay.

The Queen's English – Coming soon, Gub'nor!

Australian – Turning workplace culture upside down, down under!

Canadian – This is in progress, eh. Sorry for the delay, buddy.

Hawaiian Pidgin – Kimo's first translation was all hammajang.

Philadelphian – The jawn was all like jawn, bruh.

And if you didn't laugh at this bit of silliness, go directly to Chapter 7 on the importance of humor in the workplace.

Dedication

Thank you to the people out there who showed me what great leadership looks like in the workplace and for setting the tone for this book. Also, a special thank you to those who didn't get the culture right and led in ways I keep in mind, hoping to help other workplaces avoid similar pitfalls. You know who you are.

A special nod to the pioneer Dr. Martin Seligman, who changed the world of psychology by founding positive psychology alongside other visionaries. This new discipline has altered our understanding of human happiness and created numerous studies, tools, and resources that have transformed so many lives, including my own. Finding positive psychology and putting the research into practice has changed my life and my ability to serve others on their path toward a more fulfilling life.

Thank you also to Dr. James Doty for inspiring me to chart my course and to remember his own life story and his many accomplishments despite a tremendously challenging upbringing he transcended.

We all have the opportunity to transcend.

The Book Format

The unsolicited advice I received on the book format was wildly diverse. One tidbit included making sure the book was at least 250+ pages. I've read the workplace culture tomes cresting 250 pages, and they just don't need to be that long. My initial approach was to just write 160 pages worth of distilled content and bookend it with 90 pages of crosswords, sudoku, and coloring pages to reach 250 pages total.

When I suggested it, the publisher looked at me like a puppy hearing a new noise for the first time. Then he collected himself and said, "No." The editor made me remove those colorful pages from the final book, but you can get a coloring page inside your free Little Book of Workplace Happiness toolbox at:

https://www.focusonthe40.com/toolbox

HOW TO USE THIS BOOK

1. Accountability Matters: Read a section; try an activity alone or with your partner, friend, or team; and commit to the process. Set aside a night of the week, a coffee break, or some other time you protect. New habits form slowly, and breaking old habits takes time.

2. Jump Around: Try something that piques your interest. Though the book has a sequencing to the layout, the chapters stand alone. Find a chapter that intrigues you. The broaden-and-build theory developed by Dr. Fredrickson shows how interest sparks our urge to explore. Enjoy the process, because finding joy in trying something new is easier to sustain when it's fun and energizing.

3. The Book Is Sciency but Not Nerdy: At times we'll give you a nugget of science that can be easily applied. Case in point: I just mentioned a theory in the previous paragraph, but the idea is to have you apply the science versus understand the R2 value from an academic study. There are links and footnotes if you want to nerd out. Just don't dweeb out. Nerds are cool. Dweebs? Not so much.

4. Toxicity is Real: The final sections of this book are about creating a positive workplace culture. Think about the one really, really (REALLY!) miserable person at work. Can you think of them right now? Yes, you can see them: Negative Nancy or Terrible Todd. The naysayers, those dropping anchors when you're about to set sail, the complainers, the gossipers. Ugh. They make life painful, and they can create a Culture of Complainers (COCs). The goal for this workbook is to make life painful for the COCs, to take away their power and influence, and through creating a positive culture, the power of the COCs will either diminish or they'll be so uncomfortable they'll move on. And good riddance. #amirite?

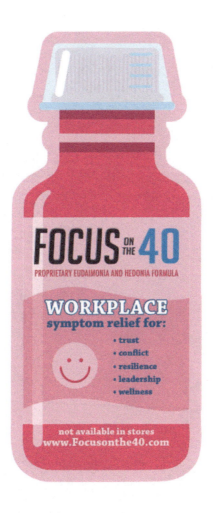

Table of Contents

"We're going to remove your appendix, and also, just to be safe, your table of contents."

PART I

Ready... Set... Wait...
Read This First

LET'S ACTUALLY START AT zero by debunking what you think you might know about happiness, and specifically money and success, and then we'll dive into what we know about how to create happier and more productive workplaces.

Why Work Stinks Like Bad Kimchi

HOW HAPPY ARE WE AT WORK? Not very. Next chapter. :/ Womp! Womp! All kidding aside, a few statistics of importance from some of the leaders in workplace health and performance:

- 44% of employees experienced a lot of daily stress during the previous day—an all-time high and even higher than during the pandemic, according to Gallup.[1]
- 21% of people are engaged in their work.[2]
- 76% of people are reporting symptoms of mental health conditions at work with 84% saying work was the cause.[3]

Yikes! It's ok for work to be hard. But we've got a lot of work to do to make work something supportive to our health and fulfilling, even though work will—and should—have challenges.

Things are bad. Like when kimchi goes bad—look out! A toxic work culture stinks, not literally, but you get where I'm going. Good culture, like kimchi, is alive, robust, and flavorful. In this book, we'll show you what it takes to keep creating the right conditions for a thriving culture. And sorry, no, we don't have any kimchi recipes, but I do make a mean kimchi and lap cheong fried rice.

And let's liberate you from idealism. Quit chasing perfection. A great job and a great workplace are an exceptional accomplishment. By that we mean those workplaces are exceptions to the (low) standard, so celebrate great culture, invest in going from "good to great," and don't hold yourself accountable to some fantastical Instagram post.

And let go of this: "If you find a job you enjoy, you will never work a day in your life." #poppycock #bovineexcrement

Quit chasing the perfect job or looking for the highest purpose or calling in your work as the end all. If you've found perfection and a calling, revel in it. That is, again, exceptional and rare. For some people, a job or career is all they want. Money is a means to an end for a larger purpose outside of work. Meet your employees where they are. Trust helps in getting to that very unique truth.

The Great Resignation Is a Symptom

So why are we so unhappy at work? Buzzwords like *quiet quitting* and *loud loafing* (ok, I made that one up) are the new workplace jargon. We have an interesting COVID-induced hangover that changed our perception of and relationship with work. And it's not going away.

According to recent Pew Research Center findings[4], people moved on for better pay most frequently, which is typical. But after compensation, people look for more from their workplace environment, including opportunities to advance, flexibility, and balance. The Pew Center data presents several opportunities for workplace shifts that cost little to no money.

1. **Advancement**: People surveyed want to grow and advance, and this is no surprise. A good dose of what is called challenge stress, and micro-leadership tasks can combat apathy and create investment by employees.

2. **Flexibility**: Offering job crafting and discretion gets your staff empowered and gives them a sense of control. Humans love control, and as a bonus outcome, control builds trust. Trust is core to deepening relationships, and strong workplace relationships are great for retention.

3. **Disrespect**: Disrespect is about misunderstanding and assumptions. In my workshops, we show teams their leadership diversity and how to lean into what makes each of us great and to find comfort tapping into different leadership styles.

Wrapping it up. If you make your employees happy—which is the combination of satisfaction with compensation, engagement, fulfilment, challenge, and connection—they will give more than you ask of them. Remember the stat on how low engagement is? 21%! More importantly, engaged employees with leaders they trust will want to stay and won't jump for pay increases less than 20%.[5]

Ya get it? Ya got it? Let's move on!

Expecting Investments in Workplace Happiness

This expectation comes from three different groups, some internal, some external:

1. **Employees:** As employees are selecting their workplace, they are looking for, or even requiring, a corporate commitment for the workplace to "be good" to their people and the greater world. This is especially

prevalent in younger populations, who are coming to expect their workplace to have a corporate mission that isn't all about the bottom line. The term *triple bottom line* of people, profit, and planet was coined a while ago but is increasingly a differentiator, if not a full-on requirement, for some employees. And if you're trying to be attractive to workers, you're creating a competitive advantage by making moves forward toward a balanced triple bottom line.

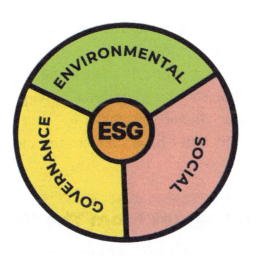

2. **Consumers:** Consumers are increasingly looking for businesses committed to corporate social responsibility (CSR), which includes how you treat your people. CSR practices are generally considered to be how a corporation commits to their choice of voluntary efforts without a standard prescription of what constitutes a "good" commitment to CSR. This is changing though, and there are a variety of ethical standards and accrediting agencies replete with their stamp of

approval in the form of a logo found on many ethically produced products. Consumers are increasingly aware of fair trade, cruelty free, B corps, and 1% for the Planet as "good" companies, and now third-party accrediting organizations have crafted a more robust CSR Accreditation, which gives more rigorous criteria for a balanced triple bottom line. Side note: one of my favorite resources for shopping is the Better World Shopper, which can guide ethical consumerism through its rating system for both the services and products of larger corporations.

3. **Investors:** Investors are also watching! Publicly traded companies are going deeper to justify investment in different investment pools and use the acronym ESG for environment, social, and governance. Organizations like the Global Reporting Initiative and Dow Jones Sustainability Index have standardized the reporting on ESG efforts.

 A Nugget From The Nerds

"Investors are increasingly looking for companies that are not just profitable, but that also operate with a sense of purpose."
—**Larry Fink, CEO of BlackRock**

The "social" in ESG includes "training and education" programs for advancing employee skills to equip employees to grow within their organization through advancing skill sets, which also support them in meeting the new demands of a changing work environment. Employees want to advance and grow, and more-skilled employees contribute to employee satisfaction and engagement, correlating strongly with improved performance.

Happier employees grow and perform better. So, let's transition to where people are misled and then dive into the meat of happiness. Which, if happiness were meat, it would be bacon. I digress.

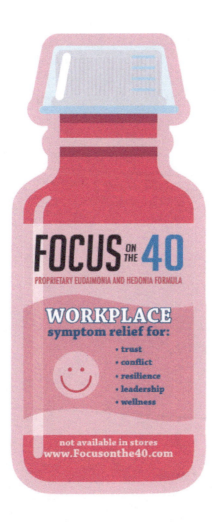

Myths & Truths About Happiness

SO, WHAT REALLY IS happiness, Tony? First of all, never call me Tony. I go by Anthony because Tony and Poponi together are a wee bit too comical for people to take me seriously. I mean, it would be nice to not be known as "The Other Tony" in leadership. I'm coming for you, Tony Robbins. Again, I digress.

Happiness has lots of definitions; there are websites full of quippy quips and quotable quotes from throughout the ages of humanity. Happiness researcher nerds in the field of Positive Psychology don't specifically measure happiness and instead look at "life satisfaction" or "subjective well-being." Ah, nerds, I love ya.

Does it really matter how we define happiness? I say YES. I even typed it in ALL CAPS like my grandmother's emails! Let's use this quotable quip as a starting point called (big reveal music!):

> "Happiness is not the absence of sadness, nor soaring emotional heights of ecstasy...it is mildly pleasant, common but not permanent and includes some satisfaction with most aspects of life."

> —Robert Biswas-Diener & Ben Dean, *Positive Psychology Coaching*

In summary, contentment. In between those natural highs and lows, we should come back to a place of contentment. We're not really meant to feel euphoric all the time without achieving enlightenment or without the use of Schedule I drugs. Aim for contentment instead. Kinda nice, right?

Here's some additional context for contentment using the three Ps! Do you live a life where you have *purpose*, *pride*, and *pleasure*? That triad of words was uttered by researcher and author Dan Buettner, founder of Blue Zones, which studies both the happiest and longest-living communities on the planet. A simple triplet of Ps but very much to the point. And we'll explore purpose in our final chapter in this book.

Can you look at your life at the scale of a day, a week, a year, a decade and say you have purpose, pride, and pleasure?

Ok, so wrapping the definition of happiness up with a rap! If the hip-hop artist Naughty by Nature, famous for their song "O.P.P.," could rewrite the song (I've suggested it; they declined) on happiness, maybe it would be P.P.P. Something like this:

"P.P.P., how can I explain it?
P is for Pride in life and how we frame it.
P is for Pleasure, a smile makin' dimples
The last P, well that's not that simple.
Purpose. A focus on the life you're livin'
A life of service will keep you driven.
Bus' it."

So, I guess I'm down with P.P.P. (Yeah, you know me.)

Happiness Is Like Reading Greek

Ok, you don't really need to read Greek to get this next part, but we're going to dive back into some Greek terms that are relevant to happiness today: *eudaimonia* and *hedonia*. "Quit speaking Greek, Tony!" Ok, ok. Take it easy, bro.

The great Greek philosopher Socrates died for his positions, as did Optimus Prime, and some say he didn't die—he just transformed. Oh wait, I crossed boundaries in the multiverse there. Socrates is the right philosopher for this section, and he broke happiness into these two distinct parts, translated in English, to: fun and purpose.

In the image on the next page, fun is on the y-axis, and that's hedonism. Vacations, comedy shows, travel, and laughter. That's the fun stuff, but the fun stuff can be fleeting in the happiness it provides (more on this very soon!). Now, you should definitely craft your life to have the fun stuff; just don't forget the other axis—purpose. Purpose includes the hard stuff like growth, change, mastery, ethics, values, and service.

Human beings are incredibly unique, and each of us has a unique formula or algorithm to living the fulfilled life found up in the top right quadrant of the image.

And our work can have both parts. In the following chapters, we'll explore the power of the fun parts, like workplace humor, relationships, and happy hours, and also where this purpose-focused element of happiness is available through overcoming challenges, the impact of teamwork, the energizing power mission, and the discomfort of growth.

Happiness Within Our Control

So how do we craft this fulfilled life, and how much of this happiness is within our control? I'll explain with a pie. Do you like pie? Oddly, some people don't like pie. I know, crazy.

What we know about someone's individual happiness score is surprising to—and energizing—for me. Researchers have approximated your happiness score, which is more of a range of happiness scores you'd report over time, into three segments, or slices of the pie.

Slice 1: This slice of the pie is pretty large and driven by our genetics, which affects our initial happiness range by roughly 50%. Some of you are asking, "But what if I have miserable parents?" Well, I'm sorry; you began with a lower starting point. The good news? Your happiness is malleable and can be changed! We'll share more on this in a moment.

Slice 2: This small piece of the pie is mind blowing in how little this segment matters and how much misguided emphasis we put on this slice. We now have massive datasets of information on where the happiest people live and what the happiest people do with their lives, and we know a ton about them as individuals and the circumstances in their lives. We know their age, orientation, religion (or lack thereof), wealth (or lack thereof), education (three times would be too many), relationship status, career path, ethnicity, number of kids, etc. Here's the crazy part. All of these characteristics combined (all of them!) only account for 10% of the variation in how happy someone is. BOOM! So quit thinking a change in life circumstances affects your happiness.

And since you're likely wondering, money can't buy happiness. The absence of money can cause suffering. We'll dive deeper right after this. The big point? Don't focus on changing these circumstances, as they only affect up to 10% of how happy you are in aggregate.

Slice 3: So, if you're doing the math, you've landed on the third segment. Yes, 40%, and this segment is all about intentional actions and choices you make. And as the name suggests, put your Focus on the 40%.

 A Nugget From The Nerds

"The very good news is there is quite a number of internal circumstances... under your voluntary control. If you decide to change them, none of these changes come without real effort, your level of happiness is likely to increase lastingly."
—Dr. Martin Seligman

These are things you can control in everyday life, which we'll explore through the rest of this book in the form of opportunities available to us through intentional choices and actions at work. And a note on the science of Positive Psychology: researcher Dr. Sonya Lyubomirsky and others have now questioned if 40% is the correct segment size, so treat this science as evolving. I'm sticking with the brand Focus on the 40© because Focus on the 39.4 doesn't have the same ring to it.

Ready to get your baseline score for happiness? Scan the code on the next page to take this free assessment called the Authentic Happiness Inventory. Once you take the test, revisit it from time to time to see how your score changes over time as you make moves toward greater happiness:

Scan to take the Authentic Happiness Inventory

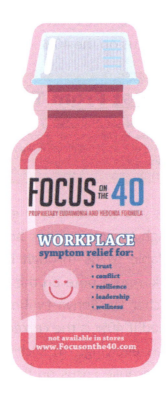

Myths About Money & Happiness

WE KNOW A LOT about the relationship between money and happiness and success and happiness, so let's tackle both of those paired subjects here.

Can money buy happiness? The answer is...[drumroll please]...kind of. Sorry, I know that's not a very fun answer. Simply put, money can buy cheese, and cheese makes me happy. As with most subjects related to human happiness, the nuance is important. Let's start with this: Would you like more money? And if you say yes, do you know why? Hold on to those thoughts, and now let's explore a few key findings.

We know the absence of money can contribute to unhappiness and a lack of peace of mind, as well as psychological and physical safety. For those living at the level of poverty, especially in third world settings, an increase in money can provide access to basic needs like nutritious food, shelter, clean water, and life-changing medical access most of us take for granted. For example, a change in access to prenatal vitamin B can be life altering for both mother and child, and vitamin B is inexpensive, as are most antibiotics. Making an extra $3 week can remove significant detractors from our happiness for some people in this world.

But that's not likely you. You're reading my book, and you likely have some of the basics at the bottom of Maslow's hierarchy covered. The Beatles quipped "Money Can't Buy Me Love," and in the US, buying love is illegal, at least in most states (looking at you, Nevada). If you're working seventy hours a week, you might be making some coin, and you better love what you do because that imbalance is affecting your ability to have time for the things and people you love in life or could love but don't have time for.

Are lottery winners happier after winning the lottery? Are people stricken with life-altering calamity less happy? Yes! But both life changes can have only temporary impacts to your happiness, and then the effects of both of these "good" and "bad" events fade. And a side note, if you're a multimillionaire or billionaire, why are you even playing the lottery? You're making the odds worse for the rest of us by 0.000000004% by buying a ticket.

There Is Always a Bigger Boat

Is the money you want for more things? People who use money for nonmaterial things benefit more. A Gallup World Poll study of people from many countries and cultures found that, although higher income was associated with higher life evaluation, it was the nonmaterial things that predicted where more money led to an experience of greater well-being (e.g., learning, autonomy, respect, social support).

Here's why: The human brain adapts to whatever contributes to our present state of being. The process is called hedonic adaptation[6]. And we adapt more quickly to material things and less to experiences and relationships. The quick takeaway: buy more airline tickets to travel with someone and fewer TVs. This message is not sponsored by the Airline Industry Association, and though the author has asked to be sponsored for the above statement, "The Association" has consistently, swiftly, and assertively declined. Big point: don't get stuck on the treadmill thinking happiness is always ahead when you get the next thing, as those things fall into the 10% piece of the pie, and you're delaying happiness at the same time.

Let's go deeper with a five-character insight and a five-character technique on how to get off the hedonic treadmill. First, the five-letter insight: TIABB! Imagine you own a yacht; it's shiny, sixty-five feet long, and sleek. Your yacht is filled with friends, family, and even enemies you've invited just to watch them turn green. Not from seasickness—yachts have stabilizers to limit sway—but instead these enemies are green from envy. You stand on the main deck, moored offshore of an island with pristine white sands, your unfocused attention taking in the moment. The chatter of your guests mixes with the sounds of the pale-blue waters of the Mediterranean, and you sip a cool cocktail. And then your gaze narrows along the shoreline to note the other yachts moored nearby. Each yacht is successively bigger in sequence than the last yacht. The final mega yacht is big enough to be a cruise ship and large enough to make your luxury yacht look like a dinghy. Your cocktail suddenly tastes less satisfying, the waters a little less pleasing, and the phrase *"Oh, that yacht would be so much nicer"* enters your brain. You've been struck, not by an iceberg, as you're in the Mediterranean, but instead by TIABB!

TIABB = There Is Always a Bigger Boat.

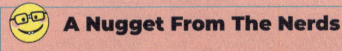

A Nugget From The Nerds

"When good things happen, we bake them very quickly into our baseline expectations."
—**Dan Harris, 10% Happier**

So how do we combat the five-letter trap of TIABB? The technique has five numbers: 12345!

Each day my phone chimes at 12:34 pm. The reminder says 12345, and the technique is a gratitude exercise shown to have lasting impacts on happiness. At 12:34 pm I say five things in my life, big or small, I am grateful for. I express gratitude for things, experiences, people, food, sunshine, warmth, or coolness. Little moments and big things all work for this technique, and we adapt more slowly to things when we express gratitude for them. Like "I sure love my adequately sized yacht!" Try the technique for twenty-one days with a goal of five out of seven days a week, and you're rewiring yourself to find more joy in what you already have in life versus what you might want.

A Resource: Gratitude Journal

Find your Gratitude Journal inside the Toolbox

Full Circle on Money

Back to our original question on money: Why do you want more money? Moving up the corporate ladder can mean more money, but it can also mean longer work hours, less flexibility and freedom, and more stress.

Are you making more money now than you did in the past? And if so, are you happier now? My answer is yes to both. Yes, I'm making more money, and I'm way more content with my life today than before. Money for me has both external and internal values. Externally, I'd like more money to allow for more generosity, both toward good causes and good people like my parents and family.

Internally, I'd like to have "nice" experiences like travel to foreign lands, music festivals, personal-development trainings, and just plain fun! But you know, TIABB.

So, ask yourself again: Why do I want more money? Can money buy me more time, more peace of mind, or better life experiences? And as the fantastic Rich Litvin asks:

"If you want more of something, what are you willing to give up to get more?"

Get clear on your answers, and you'll find the framing on "why more" or "no more!" both liberating and energizing.

Truths About Success
& Happiness

HOW DO YOU DEFINE success? Is success a metric tied to money? It was powerful for me to unwind the connection between the money I get paid for the work I do and the impact of the work I do. Some of the most fulfilling work I do is the lowest paying or even volunteering.

According to research by Michelle Gielan on success and happiness, there are three elements that are excellent predictors of your success.[7] Fortunately, these three success factors behind success are all Focus on the 40© approved because you have the ability to influence each factor!

1. **Optimistic Mindset**: Optimism has two parts! (1) A belief of a positive future and (2) your own agency in creating this positive future state. Optimism can be a natural character strength but can also be learned and developed into a strength.

2. **Social Support**: Support comes in three forms, and your network of support can be within the workplace or outside of it. Support can lift you up when you struggle, celebrate alongside you, provide shortcuts to solving new challenges, and also be in the form of direct acts. Investing in your social network is incredibly important! Social support requires effort, but life-enhancing relationships come from choosing and cultivating the right support systems and friends.

I use a professional coach, a therapist, and mentors to provide me with multifaceted support.

3. **Positive Engagement**: How do you react to stress, new challenges, and setbacks? Your mindset around these aspects of work affects how quickly you adapt and bounce back.

Curious about your own happiness scores? This activity, called "Batteries of a Balanced Life," looks at your life's different domains as interconnected batteries. Using this tool will support you in setting a baseline of your happiness scores, get you thinking about what a diverse and fulfilling life looks like, and is a wonderful tool to use to reflect on how things have changed over time.

Find Batteries of a Balanced Life in the Toolbox

Negativity Bias

We've spent a lot of time discussing happiness because happy employees are more productive, more creative, and better at problem-solving than their unhappy peers.8 What about negativity and stress? Do they have value? Absolutely! Negativity and stress are potentially valuable as bits of information we can act on and resolve these negative feelings so they will go away. Stress and negative emotions have helped us survive. But, when we are constantly living in a stressed-out environment, we are undermining ourselves. So, success starts with a positive mind. A stressed-out brain is up to 31% less productive, less creative, and less innovative.

A Nugget From The Nerds

"It turns out that our brains are literally hardwired to perform at their best not when they are negative or even neutral, but when they are positive."
—**Shawn Achor**

Ok, here's your brain in a nutshell. Some people have brains that could fit in a nutshell it seems, but that's not what we're talking about. The brain has two motivations: survival and procreation. Your brain wants to survive because, let's be honest, you're awesome, right? Second, your brain wants to help you pass on your genes through the process of procreation. What's procreation? Google it; I mean, we're talking about sex, but don't Google sex. And if you do, definitely don't click the videos tab at work. #HRViolation

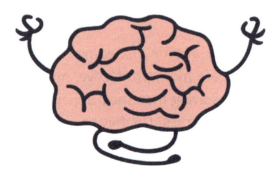

We've already shared that the brain adapts to pleasure and pleasing things. When we do something good, our

brain rewards us. Interestingly, we don't adapt to negative emotions as quickly. Our brains perceive threats and fears to have more value toward our survival than positive feelings. Notice that I used the word *perceive*, because our brains are operating in a digital world with a Windows 98 operating system. Negativity kept this old-school brain we inherited from our ancestors alive. Fortunately, *Homo sapiens sapiens* means "the clever human," thus we can transcend the perceptions, motivations, and thoughts stemming from our ancestral wiring.

What's extra surprising about negative emotions? Once we resolve physical threats in our existence (food, shelter, safety), we move on to resolving social threats, and we perceive social threats as equally important to our survival and therefore default to being equally stressed out. We'll talk about psychological safety in the next section, but for now, realize getting kicked out of the tribe at work scares our ancestral brain. Groups helped us survive and getting kicked out of the tribe likely led to death. Belonging to groups matters. And negative emotions affect our physiology and psychology for a lot longer and more intensely than positive emotions.

A TABLE FULL OF NEUROCHEMICALS

NEUROCHEMICALS OF POSITIVE EMOTIONS	ARE PRODUCED IN MOMENTS OF...
OXYTOCIN	trust, bonding, touch, positive social interaction
DOPAMINE	task completion, getting rewards
SEROTONIN	recognition, pride, accomplishment, status, respect
ENDORPHIN	laughter, exercise, crying

Good feelings don't last, they're driven by neurochemicals, and once they metabolize, the good feelsies go away. Positive emotions fade naturally because our brains briefly celebrate the good things we've done, make us feel briefly good about the good things, and then start thinking about the next thing. This is why we struggle with not enjoying the moment and quickly shift our focus on the future with a bias toward negativity. You can actively expand the positive emotions available from the present (savoring), remembering the past (nostalgia)[9], and being excited for things in the future (anticipation)[10].

A Nugget From The Nerds

"Our species is misnamed. Though sapiens defines human beings as 'wise,' what humans do especially well is to prospect the future. We are Homo prospectus.... A more apt name for our species would be Homo prospectus, because we thrive by considering our prospects. The power of prospection is what makes us wise."

—Dr. Martin Seligman

You might be thinking, "You're killing me, smalls!" because the overall message is that we're wired for negativity. Fear not; you can rewire your brain to trigger more of the positive neurochemicals (see table on previous page) and be a "wise human" that realizes those feelings are going to go away.

Mental Fitness. The first step is to build awareness around patterns. When do you get bogged down, anxious, upset, and angry? Identifying the root causes of negative emotions and patterns is a start. Then you look to interrupt those patterns before they get out of control and turn into The Big 3: overthinking, catastrophizing, and rumination.

When you're stuck in a negative state, try the following:

1. **Say Stop**: Literally say "Stop!" out loud. You're now aware of the tumbling around in your brain, and interrupting the pattern comes next.

2. **Get Up & Move**: Get up and get distracted by movement. Put all your attention on your movement. Just five minutes of movement can serve as a reset.

3. **Ask Yourself**: Your brain's tendency toward ruminating over things is valuable—to a point! When you're overthinking and especially focused on potential negative outcomes, ask yourself, "Is this useful?"

Part of improving your happiness is about removing sources of negative emotion in your life. If you're curious about taming "The Big 3," grab this free resource called "Get Happy Now!"

Scan to download Get Happy Now

PART II

The ~~Easy~~ Easier Parts of Workplace Happiness

NOT MANY ASPECTS OF happiness in the workplace are actually very easy, but there are certainly elements easier to embrace and then build upon. In this section, we'll focus on well-being, humor, and strengths, before addressing the harder-to-tackle challenges in our final two sections of the book.

A Foundation of Well-Being

THERE'S BEEN AN EXCITING framework released by the surgeon general that dives deep into well-being at work. The framework[11] defines five "essentials," and certainly without these essentials as a foundation, a workplace has little chance to provide for the well-being of its teams. And consider a foundation as just that—something stable to build on.

Five Essentials for Workplace Mental Health & Well-Being

Centered on the worker voice and equity, these five Essentials support workplaces as engines of well-being. Each Essential is grounded in two human needs, shared across industries and roles.

- Protection from Harm — Safety, Security
- Connection & Community — Social Support, Belonging
- Work-Life Harmony — Autonomy, Flexibility
- Mattering at Work — Dignity, Meaning
- Opportunity for Growth — Learning, Accomplishment

Worker Voice and Equity

Office of the Surgeon General

Essentially, a bad workplace offers up an emergency life raft full of holes to those trying to survive. And we clearly know the absence of these essentials for well-being has massive ramifications on productivity, recruitment, and retention.

As with many aspects of workplace culture, some have hard costs, like providing living wages, paid family time off, and training. Many other aspects of the framework cost little to nothing and are about establishing cultural norms showing a commitment to well-being. In a metaphorical sense, the framework's approach establishes a safe vessel in which we can work.

The framework doesn't go so far as to drive home some of the deeper impacts of how well-being is a precursor to high-trust cultures and high-performing teams. After all, he's a surgeon general, not the czar of culture. But in today's climate, with workplaces trying to do more with fewer people and a decline in engagement at work, a focus on well-being can serve many of the same purposes.

A Better Vessel Attracts a Better Crew

So, take the foundation you've built and keep building a better boat.

1. Put Ribs in the Boat

The ribs in a boat provide stability and protection from the battering of turbulent seas. Ribs are a combination of intrapersonal traits, like leadership grit and perseverance, and interpersonal in the form of supporting workplace relationships and a diverse crew.

2. Row in the Same Direction

Trust is again intrapersonal and interpersonal. Does your team have the abilities needed? Are they committed to the task at hand as a team? It takes time to build trust within a team—and get them to put aside their own needs and ego so they can start rowing in the same direction.

3. Give the Vessel a Rudder

Think about rowing for a moment. You're generally facing away from the direction you're heading. Do you trust where you're going even though you can't see what's ahead? Depending on where you're sitting in the vessel, you may or may not see patterns of cohesiveness in the team or the contributions of others. The captain can see the efforts of their entire crew, hold course amid swirling seas, and make course corrections, as necessary, when peril is nigh.

But if your leadership's approach is to run a "tight shipwreck" with chaos, conflict, and fear as core values, you're running the risk of the modern-day mutiny of low engagement and poor retention.

 A Nugget From The Nerds

"The most effective leaders express compassion, empathy, and generosity; communicate openly, often, and clearly; and practice human and wellness-centered leadership by recognizing the connection between individual strengths, growth, and organizational change."
—**Dr. Vivek Murthy, US Surgeon General**

So, walk the talk of effective leadership and building a high-trust team...or be ready to walk the plank if morale gets too low. We'll show you how throughout the rest of this book.

Relationships & Team Building

SOME OF THE MOST potent sources of happiness in our lives are life-enhancing relationships. And one of the hardest parts of life on this planet is sharing it with other people! I get it. Relationships are double-edged swords. Yet we're deeply wired to be part of groups, and work provides an opportunity to be part of a tribe working together. The working-together piece has evolutionary foundations, so let's explore.

Our brains evolved to support us living and working together in groups, and trust is at the core of working together and getting the value-add of being part of our ancestral "workplace" groups (survival!).

Your brain was, and is, constantly monitoring the behaviors of others to track their contribution to the group. Cheaters and lazy members of the tribe were, and are, exposed through the tool of gossip. Yes, gossip has a purpose. And if the influence of gossip were strong enough, we'd get kicked out of the tribe or the workplace, or both. And chances were, we didn't survive alone. That's why being ostracized creates so much anxiety.

Our ancestral workplaces spent a lot of time cooperatively finding food. Sharing food together was, and still is, an important way to team build and relationship build. The etymology of the word *company* comes from "com" (with) and "panis" (bread), as in people break bread with others, so making time to share meals with your team is important. Water-cooler talk is important to giving people a chance to connect informally with their colleagues. Organized team building and happy hours are opportunities for people to take their name tags off.

Managing relationships and building a catalog of trust for people requires storage, and the size of our brain is correlated to the number of people we can track and manage. How many relationships can your brain track? The answer is 147.8 to be exact, which is also Dunbar's number. We'll round it to 150.

A Nugget From The Nerds

"Hunter-gatherers live in multilevel societies, with groupings of individuals forming a hierarchically layered structure – families within bands, bands within communities, communities within tribes. The community level of organization turned out to be almost exactly 150."
—Dr. Robin Dunbar

Dunbar's number is a suggested cognitive limit to the number of people with whom one can maintain stable social relationships. These are relationships in which an individual knows who each person is and how each person relates to every other person.

Core to building trust in a workplace is recognizing the contributions of others, and humans especially crave their unique sense of contribution to the group. Our unique contribution provides status and the psychological safety to believe the group will still want us. If your business is larger than 150 people, it can be harder to honor the uniqueness of each individual. Jump over to the section on high-trust cultures for some low-investment, high-impact insights into how to keep the tribe humming along.

Humor Is More than Just Laughs

IF HUMOR WERE A FOOD, it would be a superfood. Humor has superpowers, and tapping into humor has incredible benefits! The research has shown your team will perform better when humor is part of the company culture. And fear not! Not everyone can be a comedian, and being a stand-up comic isn't necessary for you to facilitate more humor in your workplace.

 A Nugget From The Nerds

"Using humor in the face of failure can help us manage our emotions so we can learn from our mistakes and bounce back quickly, decreasing the transition time from one failure to the next attempt."
—Dr. Jennifer Aaker

Let's talk about the benefits of humor:

1. **Reduce Stress:** Stress has value...to a point. Working in high-stress environments bathes our brains in the fear-based neurochemical beast called cortisol, and the constant barrage is bad for our health and our performance.

2. **Build Trust:** Humor builds trust, and trust in the workplace is everything! Bonding is core to establishing trust, and 55% of CEOs identify lack of workplace trust as a threat to their organization's growth. Trust catalyzes innovation while also improving performance and risk-taking. Teams with high-trust cultures outperform their peers by 50%.

3. **Improve Performance:** Performance is part innovation, part creativity, part resilience, and all three are aided by humor. Workplaces with more trust are 76% more engaged than less-trusting workplaces.

4. **Elevate Leadership:** Leaders with the ability to perceive and support humor in the workplace are 23% more respected and better looking. In addition, elevating your leaders through innovation and tactics linked to trust means you put out fewer fires all day long.

Again, humor is a superfood. Humor is also one of the twenty-four-character strengths identified by the VIA Institute of Character. Humor may not be one of your strengths, but you can elevate the strength intentionally through effort. Alternatively, get a feel for your humor style in the resource listed below, and if nothing else, lean on others who can provide humor for your team. Set boundaries, of course, because what we find personally funny might be offensive to others.

Laughter won't solve all of your challenges and dysfunctions overnight, but humor is a catalyst for high-performing teams.

Take the assessment, sort out your humor style, and get some tips, techniques, and tools to add in some humor in your workplace.

Take the Humor Style Assessment

The Untapped Potential of Engagement

AT THIS POINT, no one is surprised to hear that workplace engagement has shifted downward since the end of the pandemic. Instead of calling them "disengaged workers," I like to use the term *the working dead*. Workplace zombies are a lose-lose proposition, and zombies bring awful potluck dishes to company gatherings.

One of the leaders in workplace culture, GiANT, estimates that employees are working at 60% of their potential.[11] Think about what that means for your workplace when you're already challenged with trying to find people to fill the existing vacancies you have. What if you could unleash that untapped potential within your team?

It starts with engagement! Alignment of skills and talents comes through really listening to what people are looking for out of their work.

Employees that are excited about their workplace, the unique challenges they get to take on, and the alignment with their strengths and interests are engaged employees that will do more than is asked of them. They also will become "net promoters" of your business and attract others who will be good cultural fits. And a high-performing and cooperative culture, as you likely already know, is hard to build and easy to break.

Success & Strengths

Work is energizing when you use your strengths and have work tasks aligned with said strengths. It's more enjoyable to use your strengths than to be burdened with constantly using your weaker attributes, and you're also likely to have more of an impact. By leaning on strengths, you'll see more of the success associated with these aligned efforts and trigger the upward spiral of "positive engagement" that we discussed earlier as an aspect of success. So, what are our strengths, and how can we put those to good use? We will explore this using two tools.

Tool #1: Character Strengths

Research from Positive Psychology uncovered twenty-four different character strengths that are found in people across all cultures of the world. These unique character strengths were developed decades ago, and the VIA Institute on Character has created fantastic tools and assessments to honor your top strengths and elevate your lower strengths. We recommend a strength-centered approach to professional development and suggest focusing on using your top strengths, which are highly unique to the individual, instead of focusing on your lesser strengths. However, we should know the lesser strengths capable of undermining us if nothing else as a tool to see blind spots.

A Nugget From The Nerds

"We can look at virtually any crisis and recount how character strengths came forth to not only help ourselves weather the storm, but also to reach out and help others."
—Dr. Neal Mayerson, VIA Institute on Character

The first step is to start with awareness of what your top five to seven "signature strengths" are and honor your unique mix of strengths. Using these signature strengths is natural, effortless, and energizing. And, in general, you'll be using those strengths by default—they're just who you are. The opportunity is to actively choose to use those signature strengths more intentionally and frequently in the work you do.

Take this free assessment through the VIA Institute on Character. You'll receive follow-up instructions on how to work with your top strengths and how to elevate your lesser strengths. Stay focused on the top five to seven even if you deem those lesser strengths necessary to keep you from undermining yourself.

Take the Free Character Strengths Assessment

Tool #2: Strengths Finder

Gallup and Clifton have developed fantastic tools and assessments to understand what mix of top five strengths are from their thirty-four natural talents. VIA's Character Strengths and Clifton Strengths do differ. VIA's assessment defines your core characters applicable to all domains of life, while Gallup's focuses more on talents and skills specific to workplaces. Understanding both types of strengths can highlight clusters of character and talents within our group and expose areas where these strengths are underrepresented or entirely absent.

Though the VIA and Gallup assessments provide different insights into your strengths, the concept for Strengths Finder is the same as with Character Strengths: use your top strengths as frequently as possible. Use them intentionally, use them purposefully, and use them frequently, because when you do this, you are staying in your zone of genius and using your talents to provide the greatest impact in the workplace.

You can learn all about Clifton Strengths below.

Learn about the Clifton Strengths assessment

PART III

The Hard Parts of Workplace Culture

NOW WE'RE GETTING TO the hard stuff! And the hard parts of workplace happiness are fully worth your energy and investment, so lean in, not out, when we explore what it takes to tackle the hard stuff.

The Hard Parts of Workplace Happiness

OUR BRAINS DO WELL with problems that are both static and stable. Chaos is hard on our brains—the poor things, they struggle with constantly changing problems. When the problem is static and stable, we can put our prefrontal cortex, our internal supercomputer, toward solving stable problems. We don't even do this problem-solving consciously sometimes. Our brains are cranking away in the background, and then poof, 2:00 am or in the shower, we're like, "Oh, that's the answer," often to something we're not actively trying to solve.

Chaos is, unfortunately, the opposite of static and stable. Uncertainty is the name of the game, and to the brain, the anxiety we feel is the result. Think about the game of American football for a moment. A field goal kicker's job is based on a few variables, like wind conditions and distance from the goalposts. The distance is known when they step on the field for a kick. The wind can provide mild to extreme variability in outdoor settings (waving at you, Chicago! Hi to the Windy City). The results? Pretty good! NFL kickers are typically between 70 and 85% on their conversion for kicks. Now the goalposts don't move, so one of those variables is stable, namely the location of the goalposts. Think about the complexity of goalposts that moved, without a discernable pattern, both closer and far away and then left to right. The kicker would feel, well, anxious. Too many variables in an already-challenging task! It would be chaos.

Chaos has been a swirling ball of joyfulness (sarcasm alert!) the last few years between the new and changing information coming out on safety during the pandemic and the resulting aftermath of determining hybrid or in-person work, supply chain interruptions, the Great Resignation, quiet quitting, inflation, and then a recession in 2023. Get used to it. The next version of chaos is just around the corner. Chaos never really goes away; it just changes form.

"Thanks, Anthony. Very uplifting!" you might be saying. Sarcasm alert! I get it. What we'll tackle next is building up you and your team to honor change, chaos, and uncertainty as real things impacting your mindset and, in turn, your performance. Change management is a profession, and there are plenty of resources around how to prepare for change when you know change is coming. Change can still feel like chaos if there isn't good planning and a solid framework for how to introduce and transition through change. Some things we'll explore in this section are how to make sure your leaders and team members are trusted and able to nimbly navigate the new norm! And alliterations will abound apparently!

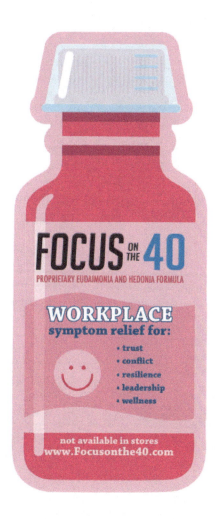

Developing Modern-Day Leaders

THE DAYS OF THE invincible, omnipotent CEO are behind us, and maybe they were never really a part of our past. Modern-day leadership has opened the door to a more humanized and mortal version of what leadership can look like. Vulnerability, humor, and inclusiveness are all attributes of the "New CEO" and new leadership. In my work with CEOs, some of the best don't know the best answer, but instead they know how to find the best answers by having diverse teams with complementary skill sets, talents, and leadership styles.

Complementary is defined as "combining in such a way as to enhance or emphasize the qualities of each other or another," the phrase *combined to enhance* being the core concept here. And intuitively we get that a small business of one hundred people doesn't need seventy-five HR directors and fifteen CEOs. I mean, someone is probably doing this but not achieving solvency. Ok, we get there is a matrix of skills and positions with unique tasks, duties, and experience necessary to "get things done," and when this is done well, we have the right butts in the right seats.

But what about those butts? What other attributes are we looking for? Companies are realizing employees are also craving a workplace where diversity, equity, inclusion, and accessibility (DEIA) are embraced and evidenced by the company's makeup. A good mix of leadership styles is also part of this necessary diversity. Workplaces need a mix of leaders concerned, of course, about the future, efficient systems, and deployment of resources and increasingly about the human side of workplace culture and corporate social responsibility.

We suggest getting a sold matrix in place to explore the diversity of your people, their skills, and their leadership styles. At the end of this section, you can take the free 5 Voices Leadership assessment and put it into a handy-dandy matrix to see where your group might be weighted disproportionately. With my clients, I look to see where alignment exists, or does not, with the leadership style and typical duties of each role, which will give great insights into how to improve engagement in some team members and where it might be improved by refining alignment.

A Nugget From The Nerds

"Leaders define the culture. Just like a gardener doesn't water every plant the same, you don't water everyone on your team the same way. You respond to others according to how they are wired, not just how you are wired. Consistency does not always mean sameness."
—Jeremie Kubicek

On the individual level, getting fluency with our default leadership style gives us insights into our uniqueness, tendencies, and weaknesses. Again, focusing in on strengths means not focusing inordinately on our less-prevalent leadership style and instead honoring what's valuable in what we bring as leaders and then making sure to invite diversity in leadership styles when solving existing problems or embarking on a new project. Inclusivity and complementary teams often expose problems and missteps before they happen when myopic views are widened to explore the full picture because of the many lenses of diverse teams.

Take the 5 Voices Leadership Assessment and start getting a feel for your leadership voice tendencies and blind spots!

Find the 5 Voices Leadership in your Toolbox

Honoring the Bumpy Road of Mastery & Growth

LET'S SET THE TABLE for discomfort and change and view change from the perspective first of how change affects you and then how you can ease your team into change. Change doesn't feel good, so start by honoring those feelings when they come up within you and expect change to not elicit good feelings in your team. But you can't shy away from these feelings if you expect them to grow.

One of the founders of the field of Positive Psychology was the late Dr. Mihalyi Csikszentmihalyi. He liked to go by Mike. He researched what he called "flow state," where we are absorbed in task. This alignment, as depicted in the image on the following page, leading to flow state is when the task at hand is matched closely by our skill set. If the task is too easy, we become bored. When the task it too hard, anxiety is the result. Staying in the flow channel means continuing to grow skills to take on harder experiences, so some anxiety is required when we take on new challenges. This type of anxiety is often called challenge stress, and I refer to this type of stress as strategic discomfort. There is value in strategic discomfort.

Flow State

People who expect and embrace this discomfort as part of the process of developing new skills, mastery, and expertise have a mindset coined as a "growth mindset" by Dr. Carol Dweck. A growth mindset honors discomfort as natural context and sees obstacles as necessary hurdles on the path of progress.

A Nugget From The Nerds

"We like to think of our champions and idols as superheroes who were born different from us. We don't like to think of them as relatively ordinary people who made themselves extraordinary."
—**Carol Dweck, author of Mindset**

Dr. Dweck's quote shows how leaders need to model their own effort, mistakes, resilience, and courage to try again after making mistakes. Research has shown leaders who share these vulnerabilities are more respected as leaders and also model what it takes to be better at anything: sustained effort. We've all fumbled along, made mistakes, tripped, and stumbled in our words and attempts when trying something new. It's the nature of trying new things and developing your mastery. Life lessons from the school of hard knocks! Ease this fear and discomfort in others by honoring your own experiences. That's leadership.

Not All Problems Are Created Equal

Remember our brains are lazy, so we want to revert to the default problem-solving strategies that have worked in the past. In many cases, we can continue to use the same ol' tools and techniques until [suspenseful music] we run into the dreaded "adaptive problems" where we're in new territory and the old way of doing things will not solve the problem. Innovation, creativity, and collaboration are all valuable in solving these problems, and an overly stressed-out brain shuts off these three problem-solving strategies. So, honor the weirdness, and keep everyone keenly aware of the value of the strategic discomfort of these adaptive problems. No one is surprised to hear that workplace engagement has shifted downward since the end of the pandemic. Instead of calling them "disengaged workers," I like to use the term "the working dead." Workplace zombies are a lose-lose proposition, and zombies bring awful potluck dishes to company gatherings.

Some of Your Ship's Crew Might Need to Walk the Proverbial Plank

And solving these adaptive problems can be incredibly valuable and part of organizational transformation. But the process can feel like driving on a dusty washboard of a currently unpaved road to a brighter future when there's a clear view of the parallel pavement of the "way we used to do things" in plain sight. We'll mix a few metaphors here. These stormy seas of change need leadership and the commitment of the crew—the entire crew. No one is going to like the change, the stormy seas, and the unsettled stomach coming from the turbulence. But you need to get everyone onboard or get them off the ship. It's a hard reality to think about losing a loyal member of a team who has value, legacy, and relationships with clients, but if you're serious about change, you can't have Heel-Diggin' Harry and Naysayer Nadine undermining the process. Everyone needs to be onboard and rowing together or else you're flotsam! Or is it jetsam?

The framework doesn't go so far as to drive home some of the deeper impacts of how well-being is a precursor to high-trust cultures and high-performing teams. But in today's climate, with workplaces trying to do more with fewer people and a decline in engagement at work, a focus on well-being can serve many of the same purposes.

Trust is critical when asking people to flex, learn, grow, and take on new challenges, and perfection shouldn't be the aim when attacking a novel challenge, so expect failures. Celebrate these mistakes as part of risk-taking when attacking adaptive problems. Trust comes first, and that's why we'll tackle trust next.

Get a snapshot of your workplace's culture by taking this assessment and sharing it with a few members of your team.

Take the Organizational Climate Assessment

Slow-Cooking Trust & Microwaving Culture

WE LIVE IN A microwave society, and trust is slowly built in the human brain. Our brains catalog the words, actions, facial expressions, and contributions of others around us. We're ancestrally wired to do so, and this cataloging takes time to build the profiles around us used to put us in the "trustworthy" or "nope" categories. And while trust takes time to build, it can be easily broken in one action you take. Quite the conundrum!

You can't put your team's trust on a microwave setting. A new team or new members to an existing team can't be expected to trust each other. If you overdo it, the microwave gets splattered with exploded food. And on the opposite side, trust is unfortunately not set and forget like a slow cooker. Slow cookers are so easy! Savory smells, tender vittles, and delicious meals—low and slow! Trust is slowly built, but yes, it takes a bit more vigilance and attention than a slow cooker. Trust is more like a backyard smoker. Slow cooking times are normal for smokers, but attention to detail on brining, basting, aeration, wood selection, temperature, and airflow all play into the final product, like a beautiful brisket! Putting the right ingredients together takes skill, intention, practice, and some vigilance to make sure things don't go awry. And now I'm hungry.

What does trust look like in the workplace? Here's a great definition encompassing vulnerability and transparency.

A Nugget From The Nerds

"Trust is about vulnerability, team members who trust one another learn to be comfortable being open, even exposed, to one another around their failures, weaknesses, even fears."
—**Pat Lencioni, The Table Group**

And don't underestimate the lack of trust in our workplaces. In a survey, a whopping 58% of those polled said they trusted a complete stranger more than their supervisor. Zoinks! This trend of low trust in institutions has unfortunately remained the norm across all institution types, including small businesses.

Building Trust Starts with You

There are two components to trust. One is all about you and your efforts and how you develop and maintain trustworthiness. Ken Blanchard breaks down trust and makes it as simple as ABCD:

1. **Able:** Do you have the skills and ability to carry out your duties? Demonstrating the ability to accomplish your current duties is a precursor to being asked to take on new challenges. Growing your team's abilities is the win-win of growing employee skills to take on new and bigger challenges with more autonomy and a win for the worker, as autonomy is a tool for retention, engagement, and fulfillment.

2. **Believable**: Do your words match your actions consistently? Or alternatively, are you the sleazy used-car salesperson willing to say anything to anyone. What we communicate in our strategic plans, internal communications, interpersonal communications, corporate wellness policies, and vision statements needs to all be congruent, or the dreaded medieval monster, the Hydra of Hypocrisy, will rise with many heads and spew gossip all about the office. Whoa, that escalated quickly.

3. **Connected:** Do your leaders care? One of the best things I heard from a client was how a specific department in their organization was struggling because one of their team members was dealing with a chronic health issue. I was excited to hear about this shared suffering, though not the suffering, because that is a connected team. Concern for others' well-being is critical to trust.

4. **Dependable**: Efficacy combined with consistency and in every direction? Direction? you ask. Direction, I say! Demonstrating dependability is important to your supervisors if you want to stay employed but equally important to your peers on your leadership or

supervisory tier of peers and of utmost importance to those who report to you. You must be dependable to everyone, in all directions. And yes, all the time. And if you know you're going to miss a deadline, let everyone know with as much advance notice as possible.

Good Intentions Leading to a Breach of Trust

I remember one of my former supervisors going around the table at a staff meeting with the good intentions of bragging about the achievements of each member of the team. When they turned to brag on me, the story shared was flowery and aggrandizing! Here's the problem: the story about me wasn't true (I was there!), and while it's nice to have someone toot your horn, the level of embellishment about how I conquered the lands and freed the people was so far from the truth that I immediately questioned the accuracy of the story of the other people around me and specifically the leader's believability in other situations. Remember, trust is cataloged by those around you, and small actions are compiled to build a trust score, of sorts, for you by each individual. Little bits add up.

A Nugget From The Nerds

"When you realize you've made a mistake, make amends immedi-ately. It's easier to eat crow while it's still warm."
—**Dan Heist**

An Easy Aspect to Building a Culture of Trust

I absolutely love going to award banquets. Honoring and celebrating people is something we need to do more often and hearing the stories about how teams of "we" accomplished things together is a common theme. We rarely conquer our foes and achieve greatness alone. One award luncheon I attended blew me away when a group of professionals in probation celebrated a returned citizen for becoming a peer advocate. The story was incredibly emotional and one I will not forget. You can read the full story on my blog.[12]

Annual awards are fantastic, and honoring lifetime achievements, unique contributions, and outstanding collaboration is a best practice. But only having an awards night once a year means recognition of achievement is too infrequent to build trust.

A Nugget From The Nerds

"Catching people doing things right provides satisfaction and motivates good performance. But remember, give praise immediately, make it specific, and finally, encourage people to keep up the good work."
—Kenneth H. Blanchard, The Heart of a Leader

Weekly staff meetings honoring recent moments of excellence are a great step! But there's an approach that will have a surprising impact if done consistently: immediate recognition. Immediate recognition reinforces behavior when it's fresh on everyone's minds and when done well is more than a "good job" and a high five. To do recognition right, it should have these components, as developed by the research of Paul Zak, and we'll model this approach as an example building on each step.

1. **Public:** Do you have small group huddles, weekly stand-up meetings, or less formal gatherings where you can thoughtfully honor this person in front of their peers?

   Example: "Hey, everyone, you know how I like to celebrate and share 'good gossip' about our team in the moment. Joan just stepped up in a big way."

2. **Peer Driven**: Having the CEO or owner of a company honor this person is a great thing to do. But realize that this can't be done by the CEO of a large corporation and have the same effectiveness as it would if done by a peer who knows their story more intimately.

   Example: "As a fellow person on the sales team, I've seen Joan navigate challenges like this before and am grateful to have her as a peer and colleague. She gets our industry inside and out and did a hard thing today with our software vendor."

3. **Specific:** Give the details of what you saw in the actions of the person so they know what you're recognizing.

   Example: "Joan, you did a great job navigating a very tough conversation with our vendor—thank you. We've all had issues with their CRM, and it's been affecting everyone, and you laid out the argument for better tech support flawlessly."

4. **Tangible:** Share what about this moment of excellence was something they can grasp in a concrete way.

   Example: "You presented the facts without emotion and kept the dialogue from escalating away from the salient points and defended our position really well with data and next steps."

5. **Personal**: Identify the personal contribution this person made that was unique to who they are.

   Example: "When you sensed the tension rising, you injected the right amount of humor to keep the situation from unraveling."

How long would a conversation like that take? Two minutes? If you need to, script out your thoughts as bullet points as you try something new. Yes, it's not always easy, but we've talked about "challenge stress" and "strategic discomfort," so lean into this and build culture with micro moments of trust. I promise you'll love how it feels.

Recognition is only one element of high-trust cultures. Transparency is another core element, and only 33% of employees surveyed strongly agree that "my company would never lie to our customers or conceal information that is relevant to them." And transparency also means sharing internally with your team—both the good news and the bad.

You can explore transparency, recognition, and the other aspects of high-trust cultures using this free assessment of your workplace, and you'll get a free resource as follow-up, with tips and insights on actions you can take to get the backyard smoker of trust cooking.

Take the High Trust Culture Assessment

The Really, Really Hard Parts of Workplace Happiness

IF YOU'VE SPENT SOME time working on establishing trust and setting the table for the "strategic discomfort" of new challenges and growth, you're on your way to setting a great foundation. In this section, we dive into the much harder parts of workplace happiness. Fear not! You've done hard things before, and tackling these bigger challenges is worth every bit of effort!

Cures for Toxic Culture

DO YOU REMEMBER THE old Western movie *The Good, the Bad and the Ugly*, featuring actor and vocalist Clint Eastwood? Wait, Anthony, did you just say vocalist? Yep! A very, very young Clint was in the Western-themed comedy and musical called *Paint Your Wagon*, and he wasn't half bad! Anyway, I digress. We talked about the good and some of the bad in the previous sections, and now we're going to dive right into the ugly: toxic employees.

Are you spending 80% of your time on 20% of your people? You know, Andy Anchor, Gossipy Gina, Terrible Todd, and Negative Nancy? These toxic employees can consume a ton of your time and headspace and impact culture in an inordinate way. You can't ignore them.

And in some cases, addition by subtraction is warranted and even critical, especially in times when you're investing in culture. You can't ignore the elephant in the room when working through change management or any new initiative with naysayers who can undermine the entire process.

Dealing with Toxic Employees

Do you have an employee like this one?

- They have incredible expertise, institutional knowledge, sales acumen, or some other exceptionally hard-to-replace skill set or knowledge base.
- They often can solve complex problems, especially when there is "stuff" hitting the fan.
- They figure out solutions to the complex stuff others can't fix.
- Your external partners and clients love them.
- They are undyingly loyal to the organization and take pride in their work.

They are obviously an asset to your company. **However, this asset can also have a dark side that might look like this:**

- They present challenges to team dynamics and communication.
- They may have a wee bit of an ego problem.
- They can be indifferent to or unaware of their negative impact on culture.
- They are problem makers, and their negatives undermine their positive attributes.

In essence: They are a pain. Yet, they are an asset. They are a **Pain in the ASSet** (PITA).

This ASSet might be your secret weapon, your sales ninja, your fixer, or all THREE! And they can also be your biggest internal challenge.

Client X of mine had a Pain in the ASSet employee, and they looked like this:

- A problem solver and under pressure figures out solutions;
- Loved by the owner and clients and would fall on the sword for the company; and
- Knew the back end of the business inside and out!

Here are two options for how you resolve the challenges of your Pain in the ASSet , hand-grenade-throwing, toxic-talent superstar:

1. Fire them
2. Harness them
3. ~~Ignore the problem~~

Remember that consistency piece with trust and making sure your words and actions align? You can't ignore the problem—that's why it's crossed out. Yes, firing them resolves some of the cultural challenges (not all!) but comes at a cost to the company, external partners, and to your organization. Letting go of ASSets is hard. Ignoring the Pain in the ASSet might seem easier, but culture is a living, breathing thing to be nurtured.

If you've reached a serious pain point with them and almost let them go—maybe more than once—and procrastinated on making the choice to improve culture through subtraction of one ASSet, but you held back, then harnessing this greatness will require effort, intent, and resolve, and you can't ignore cultural issues.

Book a Toxic Turnaround Call:

Book a call inside your Toolbox

Positive Communication

Way back in the beginning of time, no, wait, the beginning of this book, we talked about negativity bias. The brain is wired toward negativity, and for many people, it's a lot easier to both see and then focus on the negative things. Yes, negativity has its good aspects, but when your communication is always negative, it can be crippling to team communication. And on the flip side, toxic positivity is a real thing, and the human brain will be alerted to toxic positivity.

Pessimism can be our default setting, just as the optimistic viewpoint some of us have as a default can create implicit bias. And "misery loves company," but ideally, misery isn't really the state of your company and the people in your workplace. However, employees can commiserate around a Culture of Complaint.

There's a balance to strike with communicating positive and negative messages, for sure, but creating space for more positive communication requires building new habits, so you can combat this negativity with a few simple tools. Here's how:

1. **Good Gossip:** Create good hype in your workplace by having a group of people committed to spreading positive messages and, equally as important, strong enough to refuse to engage in negative gossip. Shutting down gossip isn't always easy, but you can't ignore the potential impacts to culture and to trust. Create a small group of trusted people who you can count on to interrupt toxic talk and reframe those conversations before the gossip gets traction. Combatting gossip with good gossip that is fact based and unemotional will blunt the effect of those who default to complaining, often mindlessly without

the intent to necessarily harm but also without the intent to do something to resolve the situation.

Example: In one of my former workplaces, one of my colleagues was out of town for a preplanned vacation for a portion of the week after we moved to new offices. This person was around for some of the packing and moving, but not all of it, and left the new office space where they'd be working in a bit of a mess. It was understandable, from my perspective, if not perfect. But the negative naysayers in the office jumped on the opportunity to backstab this person, and it was a terrible breach of trust. I came to this person's defense when invited into the circle, and it was a hard thing to do. I also realized I was the next target for attacks when my back was turned. Trust breached.

2. **An Imperfect Ratio:** Managing the ratio of negative and positive messages necessary for honest communication is a balance. Words impact trust, and trust impacts how people receive and process the words said. A ratio was devised, called the Losada ratio, that indicates that the sweet spot for positive to negative communications should be around 3:1. This research was later debunked, so finding the perfect ratio from research isn't an option. And honestly, if I told you to use 2.9 positive to 1 negative, how would you go about measuring that in daily interaction? What's worth noting is how you go about communicating with those around you and paying close attention to the impact of what you're saying.

3. **Constructive Communications:** A fun tool to play that can build new habits and comfort with positive emotions in your communications is called Active Constructive Responding (ACR). When someone comes to share positive news with you, this is an opportunity to reinforce positive communication using the following approaches:

- Make eye contact – don't look at your phone, no typing, no multitasking.
- Be enthusiastic – match their enthusiasm authentically; don't go overboard.
- Ask open-ended questions to explore their feelings.

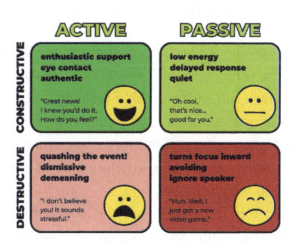

ACR allows employees to be seen and creates the sense of belonging that is so critical to human happiness and workplace engagement. Gallup has developed a twelve-question survey clearly showing the needs supervisors and fellow colleagues can make sure are met in the workplace with three questions, easily something you can help employees say "yes" to using ACR.

- Does my supervisor, or someone at work, seem to care about me as a person?
- Is there someone at work who encourages my development?
- In the last six months, has someone at work talked to me about my progress?

 A Nugget From The Nerds

"When we actively respond in a constructive manner by acknowledging we hear and 'get' the importance of what they're sharing, we show we care about the person and what happened."
—Shelly Gable

ACR is a win-win for both parties, as we are wired to see and feel the emotions of others through our "mirror neurons," which can elicit the same feelings in you as those who are sharing the positive story with you—but you have to be dialed in to really be connected and maintain this level of rapport. ACR can aid you in sharing good stories and good gossip in the workplace.

Download this free image of ACR in Action and put it somewhere where you can quickly access it when someone is ready to share some good news.

Saboteurs Abound

WE'RE GOING TO COME back to negativity bias and our tendency to worry about the things we perceive that can harm us. Again, I'll use the word *perceive*, because sometimes our brains loop back to some legacy wiring from our ancestors, and the perception might be wrong. We'll also loop back to past experiences where we've either had good or bad outcomes in situations feeling similar to those in front of us at the present moment. Our brain's recall of those past experiences can be subtle and can create stress and protective tendencies affecting how we approach new challenges, threats, and opportunities. Sometimes these protective patterns have served us well, and sometimes they undermine our success and happiness.

A Nugget From The Nerds

"Most people today live in relatively constant distress and anxiety...though the fight-or-flight response originally evolved to get us out of acute, short-term danger, most of us run the survivor brain continuously. The consequence of this perpetual stress and anxiety."
—Shirzad Chamine

By creating awareness of these patterns and assigning language or tangible personas to these patterns, we can see when they bubble up, catch ourselves in the act, and choose thoughtfully versus reacting subconsciously. Researcher and author Shirzad Chamine and his team at Positive Intelligence have created this free assessment, called the Saboteur Assessment, which converts these thought patterns into more tangible personas and also will show you which types of self-sabotage patterns are most common for you.

Take the free Saboteur Assessment!

My primary saboteurs are "Restless" and "Avoider," and by being aware of these tendencies, I've been able to interrupt these behaviors, reset myself, and get back to performing better at the tasks or challenges in front of me.

Hitting the Gym

Please, Anthony, tell us what we can do to tame these evil beasts lurking around in our heads! Fear not! We'll overpower those saboteurs by going to the gym! Not a literal gym, a figurative gym—as I've already told you, I hate treadmills and, by extension, gyms. Hard pass.

The tools employed by the Positive Intelligence team have created a series of "mental-fitness reps" designed to get you out of the saboteur mode, back to the calmer, less stressed, and more productive state of mind.

Now, we know people like choices. So, you can choose the gym routine:

Option 1: Meditate for two hours every day for the rest of your life!

Option 2: Use mental-fitness tools two minutes at a time throughout your day.

Anyone choosing option one? Probably not, not even me. So, let's play with some mental-fitness tools you can do in two minutes. When you inevitably get distracted by thoughts, just gently say, "I'm thinking," and go back to the exercise.

1. Sit somewhere quiet. Silence your phone or anything that rings, pings, or dings.
2. Both feet go flat on the floor, hands rest palms up in your lap.
3. Set a timer for two minutes.
4. Take a deep breath in through the nose and release it out through the mouth.
5. Do this three times in total.
6. Find your weight in your chair, the weight of your feet on the floor, the weight of your hands in your lap.
7. Starting with your right foot, find your pinky toe and wiggle it. Then wiggle each toe for a couple of seconds, progressing toward your big toe.
8. Switch to your left foot and repeat.
9. Go back to your breath and feel the rising and falling of your chest and shoulders.
10. Anytime you get distracted, go back to finding your weight and finding your breath.

Two minutes! Ding, ding!

You can do this exercise in so many places in two minutes as a quick reset, like: sitting at your desk; in an elevator; sitting in your car (not while driving!); before a meal; or modified slightly when walking to a meeting, before starting a meeting, or better yet, with your group to get everyone relaxed, connected, and focused.

Try this when you feel those saboteurs bubbling up, and then, as with almost all gym routines, get ahead of the saboteurs by going to the gym and building up those muscles to push the saboteurs away when they try to mug your mind.

One of my favorite activities related to our patterns of self-sabotage is to create a fictional archetype around our most prominent saboteurs.

Grab this PDF and create your "Most Wanted" poster as a reminder for those pesky internal voices and tendencies undermining your success.

Find Your Most Wanted Saboteur in your Toolbox

Conflict Is Critical to Success

IN THE EARLIER CHAPTER on leadership, we started setting the foundation for conflict. When your team has the ability to see themselves as leaders, where they bring unique strengths as leaders and weaknesses, you're setting foundational pieces. What are we building with these foundational pieces? A brick-and-mortar building, and in this case, we'll use the metaphor of a bank!

Brick by brick, action by action, effort by effort, you slowly build the bank! And sometimes you hire an experienced contractor to come in and expedite the process through focused efforts and expertise to move your project forward faster. Maybe that contractor looks a lot like me. (I'm shameless!) Once you've opened the doors, you start making deposits by layering on efforts to create good gossip, build trust, foster positive communications, and develop resilience and mastery. You're making deposits in the bank and building up a positive reserve of funds to invest in your, wait for it, human capital project.

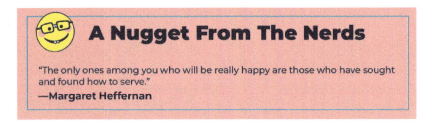

A Nugget From The Nerds

"The only ones among you who will be really happy are those who have sought and found how to serve."
—**Margaret Heffernan**

Challenges will arise, opinions will differ, and conflict is natural, and in these moments, conflict isn't negative—it's

necessary! Conflict can deplete your bank's reserves if you haven't built up your team so they can trust each other and see conflict as something not to be avoided but as necessary to moving forward with agreement and efficiency. Just like gossip, there is bad conflict and good conflict, and worrying about team camaraderie is a reasonable fear. But that's why you've spent (and better continue spending) time and money toward building up these reserves. What does good conflict look like in action?

1. **Conflict Is Not Combat:** Words matter; emotions being in check matter as well. This is about being engaged in conversation, not workplace warfare. Incendiary language cannot be tolerated or ignored. Create ground rules and hold to them. Shut down those who can't abide by these rules.

2. **Politics Are Poison:** Don't allow back-channel conversations, parking lot petitions, or politics. The forum you've chosen to solve this problem is the forum where the discussion happens.

3. **Changing Your Mind Isn't Weakness:** Opinions can be grounded in facts, and they can also be grounded in misunderstanding, instincts, or partial

information. Test your own opinions; be open to new information and to forming new and better opinions.

4. **Agreement Over Compromise:** Any commitment going forward as a compromise is weaker than a commitment made through integration. Sometimes one party has to be unhappy with what has been agreed upon by a supermajority. If they've been heard and respected, you can and need to move on. Their ideas can still be integrated as long as it isn't done as a gesture to placate.

Good conflict is robust and, when managed correctly, can build deeper bonds, trust, relationships, and camaraderie. Don't shy away from conflict if you've built the foundation and made your deposits.

Good conflict is built on a foundation of trust. The definition for trust in this context is the assumption of "good intentions" by those around you. No politics, no "good ol' boy" club favoritism and a willingness to bring forward ideas—some of which might turn out to be bad ideas. How well you foster a culture of trust is core to your ability to move toward the results you desire. Give this five-question survey a try and see how well your team is building this foundation of trust.

Team Trust Quick Assessment

PART IV | CHAPTER 16

Stress, Burnout & Work-Life Harmony

EARLIER IN THIS BOOK, we discussed the surgeon general's "Framework for Well-Being," and we're going to loop back to one specific aspect of the five facets the SG identified: Work-Life Harmony. The word *harmony* has recently replaced the word *balance*, but harmony has a nicer sound to it (forced pun!). Balance and harmony overlap, and the nuance is just that, nuanced.

Regardless, harmony, much like balance, happens at scale. Some days you have your work and nonworking life operating in harmony with productive workdays orchestrated in concert (puns abound!) and finely tuned (can't stop; won't stop!) schedules stay in rhythm, and some days, well, you look up and it's 5:00 pm, and you didn't each lunch, you're late for a family gathering, and somehow you didn't do a single to-do on your critical list for the day. Cue the haunting sounds of organs from the orchestral pit.

Some days/weeks/months/quarters/years flow smoothly, and your days are sharp (ahem), ordered, and organized, and others fall flat (cough). This musical pundemic shines a light on the true nature of many aspects of maintaining harmony—the process is not always perfect harmony in the short term. There are moments where there is a common refrain (I cannot refrain myself) of both good and bad patterns, and awareness of those patterns can give you insights on what's repeating and where you might need to interrupt the bad. When the bad patterns are repeating and regularly causing intense stress and overwhelm, it can undermine us temporarily, and in the long term, burnout can ensue.

Abating Burnout

Burnout is a commonly used term, and overused might be more accurate. The generic nature of the term can devalue the term in general and have many attributing normal stress or periodic feelings of "meh," also called languishing, as burnouts. Let's clarify the symptoms, and see where you might be with burnout, and then we'll transition to common cultural causes of burnout.

Internal

There are three primary symptoms from burnout as defined by researcher Dr. Christina Maslach:

1. **Cynicism:** This can combine pessimistic views of others with an inclination to distrust the motives of others.

2. **Exhaustion:** Feeling physically depleted, emotionally drained, or both.
3. **Ineffectiveness:** A perceived or real loss of effectiveness or competence.

And as in the image, one person burning out can have a catalytic effect on your team. Now these symptoms might all be present, might be presenting in varying intensities, or one or more may not be present at all. What we suggest at the end of this chapter is an assessment that is both short and sweet to set your baseline. And while burnt ends of BBQ are sweet, the feelings of burnout might include hints of smoke, but they're not as enjoyable as some brisket with a side of cheesy grits and stewed greens.

External

Now that we've identified the symptoms individuals might experience during burnout, let's switch over to the cultural aspects that can lead to burnout. As you read through these culturally caused aspects of burnout, think back on what we learned about trust! There is an unsurprising amount of overlap with protective measures related to burnout present in high-trust cultures, so revisit the chapter on trust if you need a touch-up!

And this quote speaks so much to how we worked during the pandemic and why it's not a sustainable model.

A Nugget From The Nerds

"The short-term strategy of self-sacrifice and speed has become the long-term operating model for many businesses."
—**Dr. Christina Maslach**

There are six big baddies of burnout culture, according to Dr. Maslach, and we'll explore those by offering up the goodies in the form of Burnout Barriers!

1. **Workload Demands:** Too many duties and long work hours with little time for recharge. The Great Resignation and recession-related layoffs have added fuel to the burnout fires with smaller teams expected to handle the workloads of their historically larger teams. Reassessing organizational priorities based on shifting staff sizes and resources is critical to preventing overloading your team.

2. **Creating Control:** There is a mutually beneficial linkage between job discretion, job crafting, flexibility, and engagement. Employees who have control over their schedule and how they do their work are more deeply engaged in the outcome.

3. **Recognition and Rewards:** Recognizing the unique contributions of your team members is a no-cost barrier to burnout. Employees want to feel part of

the whole and want to see how they uniquely contribute. Celebrate your people regularly!

4. **Workplace Relationships:** *Team building* was not a fluff term before the pandemic and is now more important than ever. Isolation and a lack of social connectedness are symptoms of unmet basic human needs in many of our communities. We can fulfill this need by creating workplace relationships, which serve as a great recruitment-and-retention tool.

5. **Aligning Values:** Workplaces with openness, acceptance, dignity, and respect set the foundation for the cultural superfood of trust. When cultural values are in conflict with individual values, you're opening the door for burnout. Mission, vision, and values statements set the standard, and daily practice must be aligned with those standards.

6. **Equity & Fairness:** Workplace equity has many layers that go beyond diversity, equity, inclusion, and accessibility (DEIA) alone. Decision-making processes, especially around promotions,

compensation, and values, should be grounded in transparency, equity, and fairness.

As with all things related to culture, Rome wasn't built overnight. A culture where barriers to burnout are built in take time, attention, and a willingness to stay the course on changing. Again, many of these Burnout Barriers are directly linked to elements of high-trust cultures, so take the High Trust Cultures test in Chapter 15 and start making moves to put out the flames of burnout.

Maybe burnout has you singed, a touch torched, or outright crispy like anything you leave unattended under a broiler for more than forty seconds. Are you curious about determining your own burnout score? Try this free assessment tool and get a grasp on your baseline.

Take the Burnout Assessment

Purpose Is the New Black

EARLIER IN THIS BOOK, we explored environmental, social, and governance (ESG) and corporate social responsibility (CSR) through the lens of investing in growing your people while making a positive impact in the world. Let's add a more personal aspect to the conversation around the mission, vision, and values statements you'll see plugged into most operating plans.

Purpose in the workplace is both the opportunity for work to provide a connection to something more than oneself and definitely more than just a profit and loss statement or revenue goals. As with ESG, workers are more than ever desiring (or demanding!) a commitment to ESG and so is Wall Street! Corporate Social Responsibility (CSR) is gaining more and more traction, and the highest demand from leadership in 2022 was for greater integration of CSR with ESG (44%), to measure impact (39%), and integration with DEI (36%).

This is a HUGE opportunity for our workplaces to contribute to social good, workplace well-being, and meaning. But does meaning really matter when it comes to happiness? Absolutely! In all types of industries, including academia, acronyms abound, of course. In the discipline of Positive Psychology, there's an acronym describing human flourishing: PERMA. PERMA was devised by Dr. Martin Seligman and other founding researchers in the field of Positive Psychology. PERMA expands to: Positive Emotions, Engagement, Relationships, Meaning, and Achievement.

Purpose has been shown to have mind-blowingly positive benefits to your happiness, health, and longevity. And as with happiness, our purpose in life shifts from finding a sense of self, to a sense of direction, to a sense of the bigger picture, and eventually to looking for a sense of how our legacy might be defined. And *legacy* is such a massive word; we can undermine our happiness and even our passion by putting too much emphasis on our purpose. Like "toxic positivity," we can have "purpose pathology." From the research on purpose by Dr. Richard Leider and others, a few things stand out from elders in our society. They wish they had found their purpose earlier in life.

So, how do we define purpose? Dr. Leider segments purpose into three parts:

1. **Having (Outer Life):** Your external experience and activity—how effectively you relate to the "having" choices in your life.
2. **Doing (Inner Life):** Your internal experience and inner activity—how effectively you relate to the "doing" choices in your life.

3. **Being (Spiritual Life):** Your invisible experience and spiritual activity—how effectively you relate to the "being" choices in your life.

A Nugget From The Nerds

"Living purposefully means choosing how you will use your gifts and talents to create more meaning for yourself and others."
—**Dr. Richard Leider**

Gifts + Passion + Values = Calling

The more you get yourself and craft your work (and your life!) to use your gifts and passions toward your values, the closer you get to a career that is a calling!

Purpose & Service

Purpose rarely exists in isolation, and meaning in life is closely associated with service to others. Service toward others is pretty clear for mission-driven organizations like nonprofits and even the public sector. For the private sector, the service to something larger than oneself can include CSR-type actions like volunteering in your community and corporate giving programs, but that can be a sliver of everyday work life...but that doesn't mean you're not surrounded by opportunities to serve. Let's start, well, at the beginning.

Can you say very quickly and very clearly what your personal purpose or mission statement is? I can!

"My Purpose is to provide joy and fulfillment in the lives of others while also providing joy and fulfillment in my own life."

Notice I used an uppercase P. That's Purpose with a capital P. It's the North Star for me and reminds me of what I've created already and what I'm actively and intentionally trying to create in the future.

I also have a purpose with a lowercase p.

"To be a ripple of positivity in small moments in everyday life."

I know little interactions matter in making others happy, if even for a moment, and I know, somewhat selfishly, I'm happier when my day includes these little interactions with people where my gifts like communication, humor, and social IQ and passions (humor is both!) are tied to my values of being a good human, a good community member, and someone who brings light and levity to everyday moments.

So, get clear on your purpose statement! And yes, there is a homework option.

Let's come back to service. When it comes to workplace purpose, especially for leaders, ask yourself this question if you direct a team:

Is my purpose to lead and develop others?

Your answer needs to be "Hell yes" or "Heck no."

A Nugget From The Nerds

"The only ones among you who will be really happy are those who have sought and found how to serve."
—Albert Schweitzer

A final exploration from Japan! We mentioned Dan Beuttner, the researcher of happy and healthy places around the world and founder of Blue Zones. One of the places on Earth with the highest longevity is Japan, and they have the term *ikigai*. No, this is not the "icky guys" from *A Night at the Roxbury*. Ikigai translates loosely to "reason for being" and, at the core, is alignment between passion, expertise, and what the world needs. Again, people with purpose, either with a capital P or a lowercase p, live longer and happier, so get to know your purpose. This image explores ikigai in four quadrants.

One of the biggest "aha" moments I've had with this tool is by exploring my role as a volunteer. I've been a board member for somewhere around nine nonprofits in my life, and I'm currently on four boards—some professional, some community based, with varying levels of involvement and even passion (looking at you, HOA board!).

When I align my ikigai quadrants, I see that my volunteerism can provide purpose in my life. Case in point, as a volunteer, I love emceeing, deejaying, and comedy. Anytime I can put those aspects into action for a cause, I leave with a smile on my face and have done some good for the world.

The four-quadrants-of-the-ikigai image can provide interesting insights into how you can craft more fulfilling opportunities at both work and in your community life. Download this PDF and explore!

The Ikigai Process

Wrapping It All Up

AHHHHH, HAIR BANDS! Warm up the synthesizer keyboard and the song "The Final Countdown" by Europe. Do do do do! Do do do do do! We're reaching the final countdown of pages for this book. We're leaving these pages behind.

"We're leaving together,
But still it's farewell.
And maybe we'll come back
To Earth, who can tell?"

Much like the [amazing] song, there are lots of repeated chords, notes, and lyrics to create a rhythm. For now, you're going to put this book aside, but hopefully you come back to the book when you need a reminder, a refresher, or to get your team back in rhythm.

A Nugget From The Nerds

"Until one is committed, there is hesitancy, the chance to draw back...[but] the moment one definitely commits oneself, then providence moves too. All sorts of things occur to help one that would never otherwise have occurred. A whole stream of events issue from the decision, raising in one's favor all manner of unforeseen incidents, meetings and material assistance which no one could have dreamed would have come their way."

—**W. H. Murray**

So, please commit! You win; your team wins.

And One Final Nugget From The Nerd I Know Best

"You gotta do the work. You'll be uncomfortable; you'll make mistakes. It'll be bumpy, and it's going to be worth it."

—**Anthony Poponi**, *The Little Book of Workplace Happiness*

And while you have to do the work yourself, you don't have to do it alone. Get support: Executive and Leadership Coaching Discovery Call.

Celebrate! You did it! Give yourself a high five! And if you're ever struggling, not getting enough recognition, or just need a pick me up, grab a copy of my free, printable, and portable high five on the next page.

Free portable high five

Booking Inquiries

Leadership isn't what you think. Let's untangle the complexity of the knot your culture is in. Otherwise, this book was all for naught, if you're still in a knot, that is. I can't stop typing puns (#cryforhelp)! If your team needs to kick up their efforts for going from good to great, let's talk. My preferred method of working with teams includes a series of group sessions and 1:1 coaching over a period of time. Rome wasn't built in a day, and culture isn't built overnight! Let's talk: book@anthonypoponi.com.

See our full catalog of in-person and virtual live programs and coaching offerings below.

See our full catalog of programs

Notes

[1] https://www.gallup.com/workplace/349484/state-of-the-global-workplace.aspx#ite-393248

[2] https://www.gallup.com/workplace/349484/state-of-the-global-workplace.aspx#ite-393248

[3] https://www.hhs.gov/surgeongeneral/priorities/workplace-well-being/index.html

[4] https://www.pewresearch.org/short-reads/2022/03/09/majority-of-workers-who-quit-a-job-in-2021-cite-low-pay-no-opportunities-for-advancement-feeling-disrespected/

[5] https://www.gallup.com/workplace/351545/great-resignation-really-great-discontent.aspx

[6] https://positivepsychology.com/hedonic-treadmill/

[7] https://michellegielan.com/resources/success-scale/

[8] https://hbr.org/2012/01/positive-intelligence

[9] https://www.frontiersin.org/articles/10.3389/fpsyg.2020.01133/full

[10] https://www.nytimes.com/2017/05/19/opinion/sunday/why-the-future-is-always-on-your-mind.html

[11] https://5voices.com/

[12] https://anthonypoponi.com/happy-tears-choices-and-the-hard-parts-of-happiness/

Made in the USA
Monee, IL
16 October 2024

67390836R00075